Psalms for the Road

C000027415

Text by Joy Cowley
Photographs by Terry Coles

Catholic Supplies (NZ) Ltd

Dedicated with gratitude to
Father Joe Keegan and the parish family at
St Joseph's Church, Picton.

Other titles by Joy Cowley and Terry Coles
published by Catholic Supplies (N.Z.) Ltd
Aotearoa Psalms
Psalms Down-under

October 2002

Second printing September 2003

ISBN 0908696-16-7
Psalms for the Road
Text © 2002 Joy Cowley
Photos © 2002 Terry Coles
© 2002 this publication, Catholic Supplies (N. Z.) Ltd

All rights reserved. No part of this book may be reproduced in any form or by any means, electronic or mechanical, including photocopying, without written permission from the publishers. All enquiries should be addressed to Catholic Supplies (N.Z.) Ltd, 85-89 Adelaide Rd, Newtown, Wellington, New Zealand.

Printed by: Hutcheson Bowman & Stewart, Wellington, New Zealand.

Contents

Introduction

In her new volume of psalms Joy Cowley has given us a worthy successor to *Aotearoa Psalms* and *Psalms Down Under*, her previous books of prayer-poems which for several years monopolised the religious best-seller lists. Joy writes with simplicity and Easter faith. They could be aptly named *Emmanual Psalms* because constantly they remind us of the ever-presence of a loving, forgiving God.

The settings are New Zealand but the themes are universal: the epiphany of ordinary events, the way nature constantly reminds us of God if only we open our senses to receive, the shalom factor in all painful aspects of living. They are essentially songs of hope.

Joy lives in a very beautiful part of New Zealand and this is reflected in most of these *Psalms for the Road*, as well as in the beautiful photographs by her husband Terry which grace each page. They are not psalms of the city. Yet because so frequently they are about people, the meaning transcends the location.

Master wordsmith that she is, Joy gives us many memorable phrases. Like the mother at birth "surfing on a tsunami of pain." Or, (in *Winter*) "like a bare tree standing alone among the dead leaves of memory".

I found many favourites. Perhaps the psalm which stood out for me was about the prayerful Grandmother, whose prayer "stitched up a tear in the fabric of the planet." Thank you, Joy, for providing another rich resource for those who seek to find a little space for God in their busy lives.

Michael Hill IC

Song for Sunrise

Hey, beautiful morning, we're singing your God song,
a psalm of seas and mountains, of empty roads
and houses yawning under a new blue bowl of sky.
It's the song of the bellbird, of steaming cows in sheds,
of freckled trout quivering in deep dark pools,
and dew on cobwebs lacing trees.
Hey, beautiful morning, stay in our wakened hearts
so we can carry your God song into the busy day.
Remind us that newness is an ongoing gift
and that every moment is potential reborn,
but if our ears become full of other concerns,
and we lose the freshness of your song,
then comfort us with the knowledge
that you will sing with us again tomorrow,
oh beautiful morning, oh song of God.

2 Morning Blessing

Haere mai te Wairua Tapu
Aio ki te whenua.
Come Holy Spirit.
Deep peace to the earth.
Haere mai te Wairua Tapu.
Aio ki te moana.
Come Holy Spirit.
Deep peace to the sea.
Haere mai te Wairua Tapu.
Aio ki nga tangata.
Come Holy Spirit.
Deep peace to the people.
Hare mai te Wairua Tapu.
Aio ki ahau.
Come Holy Spirit.
Deep peace to me.

3 Advent Calender

My heart is too uncertain for a cosmic event.
Its doors open one at a time, and slowly,
each door measuring the amount of light
that can be safely gifted to smallness,
each door uncovering an advent scene
tinselled with sweet familiarity:
a phone call from an old school friend;
story upon story read to a child;
the sun rising like fire after a storm;
a batch of shortbread for a neighbour;
an afternoon weeding in sweet earth;
a pot of tea, two cups, and forgiveness;
such small pictures, yet each one
is held with reverence like an icon.
Now there is the last door,
the final opening of the heart.
Will I see the Christ child in the manger?
Of course, I will, but why do I ask?
Wasn't he there every day?

24 December

The machines shudder into silence.
The last sheep slides down the chute
and staggers out of the shed,
giddy with sudden weight loss.
The shearers, glossed with sweat,
straighten their backs and nudge open
the lid of the chilly bin. They sit
with hands wrapped around cans,
sweet coldness against cracked fingers,
while outside a tui gargles the heat
and spits it out in two long clear notes.
The shed hand rolls a can across his brow,
and says, "It's beginning to feel like Christmas."
On the back lawn, near the potato patch,
the woman creaks the revolving line
as she unpegs clothes stiff with sunlight.
The smell of summer is mixed with noise,
pungent cicadas, loud brass marigolds,
and the grass beneath her bare feet
is as warm as cat's fur. She looks
over her shoulder and reminds herself
to dig some new potatoes for tomorrow,
and she thinks with sudden pleasure,
It's beginning to feel like Christmas.

The children and dog have been in the pool
but the dog in excitement, bit the plastic
and now the pool is collapsing,
pouring water over hot concrete.
The children run through the flood
making footprints that dry in seconds.
"Happy birthday to you," they sing.
"Happy birthday, dear Jesus."
Their grandad at the kitchen window,
remembers his own childhood.
He thinks of all the small footprints,
that have stamped the earth
since that little fellow in the stable,
and he smiles as he dries the dishes.
It sure feels like Christmas.

14

5 Cana

It was in the beginning,
the first recorded miracle
of Jesus' ministry, water into wine.
And what did it celebrate, this miracle?
A wedding. The love of man and woman,
the union of two halves to make
a oneness of flesh, of life,
a oneness of the universe.
It was a miracle of excess,
a blessing of laughter.
It was in the beginning,
and all such beginnings,
for God comes to every wedding,
to turn water into wine and remind us
that marriage is the cosmic dance.

On the Road

Please, slow down
and walk with me.
Be my companion
for a mile or two
and tell me your story,
for I have much to learn
and every pilgrim's story
enhances my own.
Speak to me of yearnings
beyond people and things
and show me the leaning
of your heart like a compass
towards true north.
It does not matter
that we borrow
from different books
or use different words
to describe the journey.
We are on the same path
whatever shoes we wear.

Behold, the Christ

It was easy to see You
in holy faces, holy places,
God made flesh in a mother's voice
or in the gentle hands of a nurse,
or the smile of a grandfather
or the laughter of small children.
Every presence of love and beauty
proclaimed your advent.
I needed eyes sharpened by suffering
before I was able to see You
in the pain of human poverty.

The man who stared at a prison ceiling,
the alcoholic mother, the hungry child,
the old woman who died alone in her flat,
the young victims who grew up
to become abusers themselves,
the people who were in despair
at their inability to make changes,
when I could look at them
through the experience
of my own crucifixions,
I realised they all looked back at me
with your eyes.
It took much longer to see You
in places of affluence and power,
in parliament or at the stock exchange,
at the helm of a luxury yacht
or residing in a summer palace
surrounded by material wealth.
But now I discover that in these places
You have the same eyes as the poor,
the disabled, the imprisoned,
the same eyes as the grandfather,
the children, the hospital nurse,
the same eyes that I see
 each morning in the mirror.
And I begin to understand a little,
just a little, of the truth
of who You are.

Haere mai

Kia ora, my friend. Welcome.
You bring honour to my house
and a blessing to my whanau.
Come in, spend time with us
and we will talk, You and I,
of good things.
You know, when I was young
I had a picture of You in my head,
a young Jewish man in a long robe,
and that is true, my friend, that is true,
but You grew with me over the years
and now I know that your whakapapa
belongs as much here, as over there
or anywhere else.
You are one of our people,
one with these mountains,
one with this land.
Haere mai e Hehu Karaiti,
Welcome Christ Jesus,
this is your home.

9 Emmanuel

Star maker,
earth shaker,
power of the hurricane,
voice of the dove,
comes to earth
in a blaze of angels,
called by compassion,
formed by love.

10 Psalm for the Road

This is not a highway, Lord.
I had expected a road better used,
better paved, more signposts,
certainly companions on the way.
Did I make a mistake somewhere
and take the wrong turn-off?
This track grows steeper daily.
Yes, I admit it's very beautiful,
and the views keep getting better,
but it seems so far from the city.
I'm not sure where I'm going.
Can't you give me a sign?
What's that? Peace? Why, yes, Lord.
This road is full of peace. It hangs in the air.
It's everywhere. You mean that's it?
Peace is the sign I'm on the right road?
Well, thanks, Lord. That's good to know,
and shalom to You, too.

Little Lights

Jesus spoke of little lights, candles, lamps,
not great bonfires, just small steady flames
to brighten some dark corner of the house.
Come to think of it, Jesus always preached little –
children, flowers, sparrows, the widow's mite,
mustard seeds, loaves and fishes. He didn't
expect people to make great gestures.
I guess he knew that little is the currency
of every day living.
So let's thank God for little lights,
the warm smile, the hug, the phone call,
a wave from a passing car, a cup of tea,
an open door, a talent freely shared.
How often, when my own candle has gone out,
has someone relit it from their lamp of kindness.
That can't happen with a big light.
I mean, how close can you get
to a supernova?

Lazarus and the Rich Man

Often I have been poor and begging
for crumbs from the rich person's table.
Sometimes I didn't know I was needy
until I saw the other's abundance
of confidence or happiness or faith,
and my heart cried out in hunger.
Often I have been given not mere crumbs
but a great banquet of generosity.
I've been put in the seat of loving kindness,
the entire table open before me.
 I've feasted on the bread of friendship,
drunk from the cup of self-esteem
and seen the blossoming of my faith
mirrored in the eyes of my companions.
Oh God, let me not forget these moments.
On those days when my own table is rich,
may I always remember to set extra places
and chairs of loving kindness
for the stranger outside the gate.

13 The House on the Rock.

(Matthew 7: 24 - 27)
You know, I have this feeling
that the wise man who built on the rock,
had previously built a house on the sand.
He'd learned that sand meant wasted effort
and solid rock was the way to go.
How much wiser that man was
than the one who built on the rock
simply because he didn't know
the sand was there.
Mind you, for people like me,
that wisdom is hard won.
I built several houses on the sand
before the message got home.
Maybe that's why I value rock so much.
At times, I've heard people say
that they don't know why God
allows the pain of sin in this world.
Well, if I substitute *sand* for *sin*,
I think I have something close
to an answer.

14 Mountains and Plains

Jesus prayed alone on the mountain,
a place where he could be at one
with his Father. Then afterwards,
he took the power of that prayer
down to the plains where people
waited for his healing touch.
We have been there in the crowd.
We've called out our need
and have felt our lives come together
in his hands. Then afterwards,
he has asked us about our prayer.
"Where is your mountain?" He says.
"Tell me, where are your plains?"

15 Pentecost

You didn't come in a great wind
or in swirling tongues of fire,
but with a touch as gentle
as the wing of a butterfly.
Yet instantly we knew You,
our recognition much older than words,
and we opened like flowers
to the sweetness of the moment.
Then it was over. The sun continued
its path across iron roofs,
birds flew in and out of the fig tree
and the neighbour's dog, nose down
vacuumed smells from the footpath.
But no, not over, for this remains,
this light that stitches all things
into a shimmering oneness,
so that we lose ourselves
in sun, houses, tree, birds, dog,
and we know as we stand here
on holy ground, that nothing
will ever be the same again.

Emmaus

On that day of rain, I walked with You,
seeing but not seeing You in wet trees,
hearing but not hearing You
in the symphony of water sounds
played by a flooded stream.
You were everywhere and yet closer
than the sanctuary of my umbrella,
closer than a misted breath.
I didn't need to ask who You were
for my heart burned with recognition.
Fearing that I would lose You, I cried,
"Oh Lord, come home with me!"
You smiled through the dancing rain,
the puddles, the grey fence posts,
and You whispered, "Ah! I am already there."

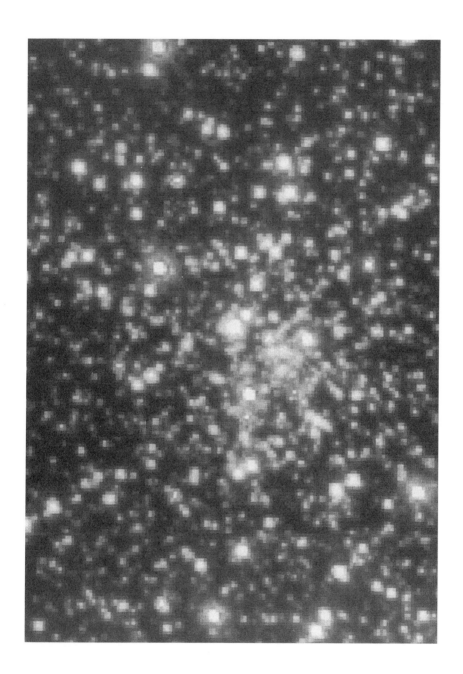

17 The Night Sky

Oh God, when I stand under the stars,
I am filled with nameless awe
at the immensity of your presence,
and I wonder how, in my daily thinking,
I can make You so small.
Oh Holy One, the All of existence,
how can I claim to know your mind?
How can my tiny words describe the Word
that brought this universe into being?
Could it be that I worship an idol
of my own making?
In your all-pervading presence, You know
the limitations of the human heart.
Have You given us this night sky,
this vision of galaxies growing and unfolding,
to remind us that we have two gods,
one that we make in our image,
and the One who made us?
Oh God, I stand under the stars,
filled with nameless awe.

Who Are You?

Precious Child, don't ever say that you are nobody.
You are not no body. You are not even some body.
You are a special, one-time, never-to-be-repeated
act of God's creation. You are unique.
Listen! Ever since the beginning of the universe,
when God spoke the Word that created matter,
ever since the emergence of life on this planet,
there has never been another being made
exactly like you. Not only that.
There will never be another like you, again.
Not ever! Think about that for a moment.
Consider your giftedness, unlike any other.
Reflect on the position that only you can fill.
Doesn't that say something to your heart?

19 God Bless You

God bless you, my friend.
May the seasons of your life be held in love.
May your winters be short and your summers long.
May smiles pour upon you, warm like the sun
and may your tears refresh like the rain.
May your garden flower abundantly
sweetening your neighbourhood,
and may your roses always bloom larger
than their thorns.
God bless you, my friend.
May your wisdom increase like a deep-rooted tree
and may peace always nest in its branches
to sing to you above the noise of storms.
May you always see yourself
in God's plan for a blossoming earth,
and may the fragrance of your truth
be celebration for all.
God bless you, my friend.

A Hymn to Imperfection

Hey! Let's celebrate weakness!
Yes! You know!
Weakness as in failure!
Let's celebrate the slips and slops,
the drops and falls and oh-ohs
that teach us wisdom
and compassion
and patience
and humour
and understanding
of what it means to be
not a human being
but a human becoming.
Let us celebrate
all those opportunities for growth
that were ours yesterday and today.
Let's celebrate for ourselves.
Let's celebrate for each other.
And while we are at it,
let us give thanks
for the mistakes
we will make tomorrow.

If we find them painful
or a bit embarrassing
we can remember that perfection
means having no room
for improvement,
no need for anyone else,
and who wants that?
Let us be grateful,
oh so deeply grateful,
that God is still shaping us.

21 The Other Sea

There is something about a sun setting
over a rim of ocean, the day dying
through a range of colours from orange
to deep purple with a touch of green
at the horizon. The hush-hush of waves
was backbeat to our conversation
about the weekend, family together
for the first time in three years,
then Steve arrived with fish and chips
and the talk turned to food.
With newspaper packets in our laps
like hot water bottles, we pulled out chips
and wondered who had come up with the name
of lemon fish for plain old shark.
I think it was Jo who said out of the blue,
"We could call this a Galilee meal."
I don't know what she meant by that,
but it made us move into a silence
all together, yet each of us alone
in a fullness of thought.

The quiet didn't last. Someone laughed
and said shark was a much neglected fish.
Didn't we know that grilled shark steak
cost the earth in Hawaiian restaurants?
Talk went on about local eating habits,
but in those few silent moments,
our boats had been out in deep water
and we had all been fishing.

Cushions and Pavlova

Okay, God, this is really deep layer stuff,
the truth beneath the truth, if you know what I mean.
The fact is, I'm a comfort junkie, and I'm not talking
about armchairs and three full meals a day.
I mean emotional cushions and spiritual pavlova,
an inner life that is soft and sweet.
In other words, I want everything to be nice.
Yes, yes, I know you're not Santa Claus,
and years ago, I gave up asking for a new job
or fine weather for a picnic, because I realized
that you knew better than I, what my needs were.
No, these demands are deeper and more addictive.
I tend to shut out people who don't prop me up,
and I shrug off the harder disciplines of faith.
Understand that this is not big time confession.
I've done the breast-beating bit before,
in pursuit of spiritual goodies. No, it's all about
being real to myself, to others and to you.
I need help, God, to get me past this addiction
to cushions and pavlova, and out into the world,
the real world, where you give with two hands.

The Open Door

Life is just one door after another,
and the thing about doors
is that they don't compromise.
They are either open or shut.
We all know the slamming door.
Sometimes it shuts so fast
that it almost cuts us in two,
and we are left in a state of grief.
At other times a door closes slowly,
squeezing us out of breath
until we have to step aside
and let ourselves be locked out.
A certain fact about doors
is that when one shuts on us
another one always opens,
but that's not easy to see.
Often, I'm so busy knocking
on the door that's solidly shut,
that I'm not aware of the other door
wide open at my back.

Maternity

She feels that she is surfing on a tsunami of pain
and losing control. She will fall and drown.
But as the wild wave bursts over her, it subsides,
and she is left whole but tired under a bright light,
someone telling her she has a boy.
It was supposed to have been a girl but that
is forgotten, as they place him at her breast,
wet black hair streaked with mucus,
face folded like a flower bud, mouth searching.
When someone dims the lights, the creases
of his eyes widen into a gaze that fastens on hers,
and she knows she is looking into his soul.
There has been a shift in the universe.
She has forgotten the long labour and pain
and before that, the weeks of waiting.
The voices around the bed, her husband,
their other sons, the midwife, become distant.
She nurses the baby and knows only
the eternal truth of this moment.
Every mother is Mary
and every child is the Christ.

25 God of the Unexpected

O God,
guidance is my friend,
and will always be so,
but may my mind
never become closed by belief.
May it always be open
to the surprise of You,
to the newness of You,
to the rush of wonder that comes
with the discovery of You
in unexpected places.
Amen, Amen.

26 Worship

We are so grateful
for the gift of worship,
for the recklessness of it,
the unquestioned giving
that makes us to throw
our hearts out like hats
to be caught and filled
by the everything of love
that we name God,
for the rightness of it,
as it leads us
out of the wasteland
and into the blossoming way
where we discover love
moving in everything
like fragrance on the breath
of a flower,
for the richness of it,
the manner in which
we are lavishly filled,
in spite of ourselves,
with wisdom beyond mind,
seeing beyond vision,
rejoicing beyond words
and the knowledge that now
is the eternity of Love
we have been waiting for.

The Eternal Lover

Stop!
You are looking in the wrong direction!
I am not two thousand years distant
but right here beside you,
my shoulder against your shoulder,
my hand resting on the back of your neck,
my breath mixed with yours
in the same moment.
How could you miss me?
Forget the history and politics
that make truth small.
They are not important enough
to be pursued or rejected.
Turn with the eyes of your heart
and see who has not left your side
since your soul took human journey.
Say my name in our own secret language
and remember what we have always been
to each other.
Lean on me, Beloved.
Trust to die into my love.

The Oneness of Being

There is no separation.
Peel back the strip of water
and see the oneness of the land
that lies beneath it.
Feel the same pulse
in the roots of northern kauri
as in the kelp beds of the south
and know the Heart
that lies behind it all.
We are not separate,
you and I and they,
born of the land and returning,
sharing its life, its breath,
its song of rejoicing.
How rich and beautiful
are the many faces
that come from the One!
Separation is the illusion.
What is known by every tree,
every bird and blade of grass,
we learn step by slow step
in the journey together,
as we gift each other
with the extra vision
that we call love.

So come then, dear friend,
peel back the strip of water.
Peel back the land itself.
Go beyond skin and images
and the knife edge of ideas
and embrace the shining reality
of the Oneness of all being.
The Kingdom is truly within.

The Broken Heart

If your heart is broken,
do not wrap it in bandages
but leave it wide open
to the weather.
Let the sun warm it,
let the rain wash it,
and let the wind plant it
with seeds of new growth.
Before you know it,
your poor broken heart
will have grown a garden
of glorious flowers.
People will visit it,
birds will sing in it
and the wind will bear its seeds
to other broken hearts.

Treasure

One fine morning, the child stood on a lawn
covered with daisies and dandelions,
and hardly dared breathe for beauty.
The grass was thick around her ankles and in it,
as far as she could see, were jewels laid out
on spring-green velvet.
Each daisy was a perfect yellow cushion
edged with white petals, some blush tinted.
Every dandelion was made from sunshine,
and some had on their faces, wet diamonds
that shivered and glittered when they rolled
onto the child's fingers.
She took a bunch of this perfect treasure
into her father and he admired every flower,
his eyes growing soft with memory.
Together, they put them in a glass
on the kitchen window sill which instantly
became a shrine to beauty.
Later that day, someone said, "Nice lawn.
It's a pity there are so many weeds in it.
I have a spray that'll get rid of them."
At that moment, the child learned
that when a treasure is judged a weed
it has no value at all.

Being Good

The voice of the heart reminded me,
"You don't have to be good to be holy,"
and I looked back on the hungry days
when my search for goodness took me
into the city of fear and the streets of division.
How often my notion of goodness
was connected to my own comfort.
How often it created an opposite image
for those on the other side of town.
Good, evil, right, wrong, us, them.
"Come," said the voice of the heart.
"Don't burden yourself with judgment.
Take from the streets of division,
the knowledge that you must leave them
to go out to the country of kindness.
Let wholeness replace your hunger.
Let the truth of Christ set you free."

The voice of the heart reminded me,
"You don't have to be good to be holy.
All that is needed, is love."

Earth Songs

The earth is full of songs, some joyful,
some angry, others full of tenderness or grief.
Everywhere there are songs and singers
who are eager to share their melodies.
But the world is short of listeners.
Yes, my friends, listeners are rare.
It's a shame when a singer must pay
someone by appointment to hear a song,
a listener who counts rhythm on a watch.
Wouldn't it be a great old world
if we saw each other's songs as treasure?
Then we could say, "Yes, please,
sing to me your song of anger,
for I too know anger, and perhaps
your anger and mine can hold hands
and do something creative."
Or we could say, "Sing out your grief.
My heart is open and it will collect
the beauty of your tears."
Unfortunately, we too, wear watches
and often we are deafened by our own songs,
tunes that have gone unheard for years.
What a pity! What a waste!
Oh God, help us to value the songs of earth
and to know every one as a gift of heaven.

33 The Desert

Prayer doesn't always flow like a river.
There are times when it's not a trickle.
My heart becomes as dry as a desert
and words blow like dust on the wind.
I remember past floods of blessing,
green growth and fruit on the vine,
and I become restless with grief,
as I search for a way back to Eden.
But if I sit still in the desert,
sit long enough to listen,
I find messages in the sand dunes.
I hear words on the hard dry wind.
The meaning of sand is patience,
waiting with a poor empty heart,
for the rain which will come in time.
The wind's voice speaks of detachment,
the distance from comfort which shows
miracles at work in dryness.
Slowly, so slowly, I've learned
the value of prayer in a desert,
and I have come to trust the giving
of all seasons of God.

Pain, Truth and Love

I asked to be free of pain
but Wisdom told me no.
She said that without tension
no living thing could grow.
She told me I should enter
this wretched pain of mine
and one day I would see it
not as evil but divine.
Whenever a cry of pain is heard
comes Mary pregnant with the Word.
God spoke into my heart
a truth I would not share.
I thought I'd be rejected
by people everywhere.
But Wisdom gently said,
"You have no cause for fear.
God provides the voice
and the listening ear."
Whenever a voice of Truth is heard
comes Mary pregnant with the Word.
Love held out a begging bowl.
I didn't know what to say.
What would there be left for me
if I gave my heart away?

"Give," said Wisdom. "Give and give.
Hesitation makes you poor.
God is Love and limitless
He takes to give you more."
Whenever a song of Love is heard
Comes Mary pregnant with the Word.

Grandmother

She never learned to read, and didn't know Scripture
but as she sat in a wicker chair, mending her family's clothes,
she murmured, "Thank you, God. Praise you, Jesus,"
and somewhere far away, her prayers stitched up
a tear in the fabric of the planet.
With a pot of soup boiling on the wood stove,
she stood at the table, kneading bread
grateful for the richness of another meal.
"Thank you," she said. "Thank you, thank you, God."
and in a lonely place, a hungry heart was filled
with a nourishment it could not name.
She said her only regret was her lack of schooling.
It would have been nice, she said, to read stories
to her grandchildren. But what a blessing it was
that they could read their books to her.
"Thank you, God," she said. "Thank you! Amen!"
When the doctor told her the news,
she folded her hands in her lap, smiled
and replied, "Life is so lovely, praise God."
He, not sure that she understood,
said she had only a few weeks to live,
and she, knowing he didn't understand,
clasped his hand and said he was very kind.

Her children and grandchildren sat by her bed,
talking in low voices and someone remarked
how soft her hands had become.
The end was so quiet, they were not sure
of the moment of her leaving, but they knew
that the angels who took her to heaven,
had to carry her just one very small step.

36 Memories

I own my memories and honour them
and give God thanks for the way
they have shaped my being and my becoming.
I give thanks for the people who have loved me,
for they revealed to me the essence of God.
I give thanks for the people who did not like me,
for they taught me how to look to my own heart.
I give thanks for moments of beauty,
for they perfumed the sacred path of life.
I give thanks for experience of the ugly,
for without it I would not have recognized beauty.
I give thanks for the journeys through pain and loss,
for they emptied me of all that was false.
I give thanks for the times of spiritual gain
for they flooded my emptiness with light.
I give thanks for all the giving
from the two hands of God,
the sweet, the sour, the soft, the hard,
the lessons that come together in growth.
For every memory, including those
I once tried hard to forget,
my heart spills out gratitude.
And now, in trust I give thanks to God,
for the memories I will make today.

Beauty

Let us give thanks for the beauty we know,
autumn colour and wet spring blossom
nature pinging against our hearts,
causing them to slow in awe,
thanks for sunlight green in a wave,
for diamond bright beaches and starry nights,
thanks for the beauty in children's eyes.
Let us give thanks for the loveliness
that is concealed from us,
the melting miracle of snowflakes,
the geometry of crystals deep in the earth
and colours dreaming in paua shells,
or life under a miscroscope,
hidden, yet when seen, so familiar
it's as though our souls knew them
long before we were born.
Beauty seen and heard, beauty touched.
Where does it come from, this delight,
and what can be its function?
Is a knowledge of beauty
the gift of God's love
that we bring into the world with us?
Is it the secret mirror of our souls?
Oh yes, my friends, oh yes!
Let us give heartfelt thanks for beauty,
God's reminder of what we really are.

One of Those Days

Yes, Jesus, it's been one of those days,
full of whining and complaint, most of it mine,
and I'm in no mood for apologies.
Let me sit in silence for a moment
to think and breathe out the tangles.
No, I'm not asking You to do anything
except to stay with me in the quiet.
Most of your friends were like me
and that's something of a comfort.
So, like always, just be there for me
while I get back my stereo vision.
Later, You can take me
to your house of celebration.
We'll have a meal together
and we'll probably laugh
about life's little complications.
Right now, they aren't small or funny.
Thanks, Jesus.
I knew You would understand.

Winter

God, God,
today the sun did not rise
on the landscape of my heart.
There is nothing to see but darkness,
nothing to feel but a cold
that goes deeper than my bones.
I am like a bare tree standing alone
among the dead leaves of memory.
Storms of grief and anger beat against me
and there is no shelter.
Why did this happen?
I did not ask for winter.
It came suddenly, beyond my control,
stripping away my comfort
and leaving me desolate and helpless.
It hurts to think.
It hurts to be.
I know that I can't turn back the seasons.
Never again, will I enjoy last summer,
but in the deep cold of frozen sap,
there is a message of a spring to come
and already, where old leaves fell,
there are the beginnings of new buds.
All I can do today, is lie still and wait,
knowing that when the greenness and light
come again, I will be bigger and stronger
than I was last year.

Grief

Friend,
I don't know what you are going through.
I've had grief in my life, but this is your grief,
your pain, and I am on the outside.
I realise that words of comfort are useless
to someone hanging on a cross.
All I can do is be here for you,
bring in the washing, answer the phone,
make a pot of tea for visitors,
hug you when hugs are needed,
and listen when you need to talk.
If you want silence, tell me.
If you want me to go, please say.
You know me well enough
to treat me as one of the family.
Friend, I can only stand here
at the foot of your cross,
but know in your desolation,
that you are not alone.

41 The Return

They say our friend is dying, and it is true
that the frail clay vessel leans back to earth,
as his soul loosens its moorings.
But his body is not yet finished.
See the light that shines in the windows
of his eyes, a light made for the Light
beyond us, and see the peace that descends
as he passes beyond the struggle.
They say our friend is dying, they who look
through the wrong end of the telescope.
This is not a ceasing but a becoming,
a leaving of this shadowed existence,
this womb, this little time of growth,
to return to the full reality of Life.
We the midwives, hushed with awe,
can do no more than tend him,
as his body gives birth to his soul.

Service

She was cooking meals and setting tables
with God leaning heavily on her heart.
"Follow me," said God, "Come, follow me."
"Oh Holy One," she answered, "I am yours.
Tell me how I may follow you."
And God said, "Cook meals and set tables."
"What do you mean?" she said. "I've been
doing just that for almost nine years.

I'm talking about a real vocation."
And God said, "For nine years
your hands have been at work
but your head has been in other places.
Be present to cooking and serving meals
and see what happens."
With disappointment and a little doubt,
the woman tried to be present to her work,
and gradually, there was a change.
She began to notice the beauty of food,
every vegetable a miracle of design and flavour.
She saw the progression of life in the food chain,
how plant and animal changed form
yet remained a part of the Oneness.
Setting a table became a sacred task,
the preparation of an altar, cloth and flowers,
fine dishes for the food, and places for guests.
Eventually, she saw cooking and setting tables
not as a chore but a vital act of prayer
which had changed herself, her meals
and the people who sat at her tables.

She prayed in gratitude, "Oh Holy One,
"I don't know how to say this,
but it seems that every meal is Eucharist."
And God said, "Good. You're catching on."

Around the Table

Dear lover of food and wine,
your laughter doesn't feature in the gospels
(writers never take humour seriously)
but your enjoyment of good times
comes through between the words
and your cosmic jokes shimmer
on even the dullest days.
Dear lover of parties and people,
thank You for the gift of celebration
and the ways your hospitality has touched us
through two thousand years of dinners,
picnics, holidays, festivals, weddings,
dances, birthdays and reunions,
reminding us that serious concerns
all too often divide us,
that love and laughter heal us
and make us one.

44 The Softness of Life

I observe how nature speaks
the word of God in parables
that support the patterns of our lives.
I watch the movement of the tides,
the cycle of the seasons,
and see how they are echoed in us;
ebb and flow, winter and spring,
loss and increased gain,
the entire universe expanding
in a sacred plan for growth,
and I know that I am part
of this oneness.
Today I held a dead bird in my hand,
stiff as a board, legs like sticks,
and I thought how rigid is this thing
we call death. How hard and inflexible.
The wind comes in from the sea
and sweeps through the green hair
of willows, and the branches sway
in the soft and supple dance of life.
But the same wind in a dry, dead tree
causes branches to break
and scatter.
Today, as nature spoke the word of God,
  I looked at the parables of death and life
and I reflected on my faith.

On the Road to Jericho

It was no five minute miracle.
These things take time, You said,
and You sat beside me,
at the edge of the road,
your hands on my eyes,
slowly and gently removing
my judgmental attitudes.

I admit I felt vulnerable.
There's comfort in shadows.
The world of light was so vast
that if You hadn't been there,
I might have changed my mind,
but your touch spoke to my eyes
and there was no going back.
As You healed my blindness,
You asked me what I could see
but I didn't have words
to describe the loveliness
emerging from the light
or what that loveliness
was doing to my heart.
It was beauty, You said.
Without the blindness of judgement,
the eyes see only beauty
and when the eyes see only beauty,
the heart knows only love.
The heart that knows only love,
You said, is in the presence of God.
I told You I couldn't see as well as that,
and You reminded me again
that miracles took time.

46 Guidance

Oh Holy One,
speak to us of the love
that carries us out of the city of words.
May the streets of instruction,
the signposts of advice,
simply serve us as guides
that lead us to the place of light
where words are consumed
by your radiance.

Incarnation

Medicine has said, "The body is a machine,
cells organised by genes and nutrition.
It often needs repair."
The Church has said, "The body is a sin,
frail, a burden to the spiritual life.
It must be subjugated."
Philosophers have said, "The body
is the servant of mental processes.
We think therefore we are."
The market place has said, "The body
is big business, to be measured in dollars.
We sell it beauty and youth."
The body says, "Listen to me!
I am the supreme gift of the divine.
I am the miracle of love made by love.
I am celebration! I am dance!
I am the pleasure of God."

48 Pilgrimage

Lord I'd like to be a pilgrim. By that, I mean
I want to be serious about the spiritual life,
regular worship, daily prayer, some effort to become
a nicer person to my family and neighbours,
the kind of thing You've talked about
for more than two thousand years.
But Lord, I'm not sure I can do it. I've read
about pilgrimage and it seems to me
that You ask a lot of followers, a hard road
and steep mountains that have to be climbed.
That's okay for holy disciples, but me,
Lord, I'm just your average tag-along.
I've never been one for steep mountains.
I know now that I would never make it.
I'm wondering, is there a compromise,
some kind of easy slope for beginners?
What's that, Lord? Oh. I see.
The problem is not the mountain.
It's the pebble in my shoes.

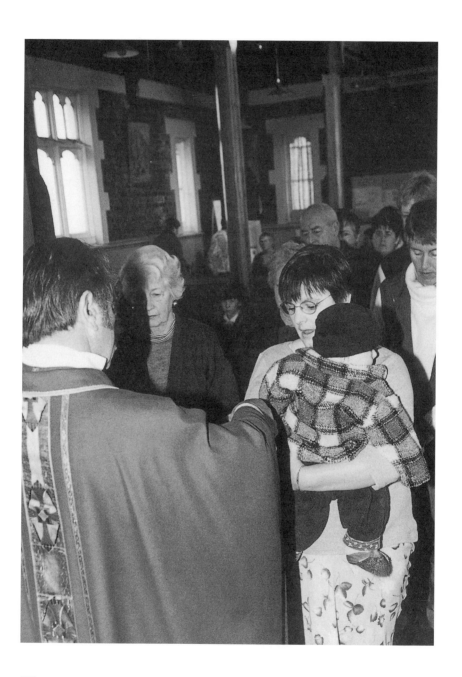

Eucharist

I am not worthy to receive You.
Sunlight slants through high windows
across a line of faces and upturned hands.
My own cupped hands are not empty.
They are brimming with weariness,
tired words of denial and betrayal.
Trade and exchange.
I am not worthy to receive You
but only say the word.
This now is the interior moment.
In a cave of silence, heads bowed,
we hold out our hearts like begging bowls
for the One who has shared many meals
with us, and who will go on giving
no matter what.
I am not worthy to receive You
but only say the word
and I shall be healed.
Now there is the hush of peace,
as we move back to our seats,
our hands empty, our hearts full,
transaction completed.
We kneel in gratitude.
The miracle is not in the bread made body
but in the darkness turned to light

The Fire of Love

Oh God,
sometimes you blaze in a radiance
that is too much for my smallness.
I burn up in the fire of your love,
my heart so aflame, that surely
it must burst in a shower of sparks.
And yet, I seek your fire, Oh God, my God,
for even in its smallness, my heart
recognizes its home, and like a moth,
seeks to throw itself on love's altar,
losing its being in light beyond light.
Oh God of love, there will come a time
when I can fly to You, wings outstretched
in the celebration of my soul's return.
Meanwhile, the longing for your fire,
is my earthly taste of both heaven and hell.

Walking to Work

I'm going to put down this thinking,
step out the back door of my head
and greet the day with my senses.
Wow! I'm breathing, smelling the air,
daffodils in a planter, a hint of dog pee,
coffee from the shop across the road.
Wow again! How come I didn't realise
that water on asphalt smells like violets?
I'm playing the game of seeing as though
I've been blind until this minute,
really seeing the ruffles of lichen
on a signpost, and the sun making
three tones of shadow on the cream walls
of the old Post Office, and glossy leaves
hanging over a wooden fence,
spotted on their pale undersides.
I'll take off my gloves and touch wood,
grit of concrete, cool leaf, soft petal,
hard steel and fluff of fabric.
What about the gift of hearing?
I reach out for the small sounds
beyond the drumming of traffic,
the cooing of pigeons, rustle of newspaper,
a few seconds of violin on a car radio.
Hey! I am feeling so alive!
You know, this is just like prayer.

The Living Christ

Tell me, are you pregnant?
No. Don't laugh.
Don't say, "Hey, you're crazy!"
Look into your heart and tell me.
Is God growing, kicking?
Remember when it happened?
The angel appeared, Gabriel leaning
on the dead-locked door, and you,
confused, said, "How can this be?
I've never been the religious type."
And the angel said, "What you believe
doesn't matter a fig. The breath of God
will come upon you. The Holy One
will fill you with life." And you thought
you were dreaming. Remember?
You're pregnant, all right.
You've got a hunger for spiritual food,
although you don't like to call it that,
and your heart is expanding
with a presence you can't explain.
You don't know where all this is leading.
You want to sue the makers of dead-locks
for the loss of your independence,
but at the same time you're happier
than you've been in years.

Relax. These are early days.
In the fullness of time,
you'll understand the mystery
of God's growth in your heart.
A bright star will speak to you
about ongoing birth,
and you will rejoice
with the love songs of angels.

53 To My Children

Stretch high,
reach wide,
feel deep,
give big,
think love,
love life,
stay open,
see beauty,
taste God.

54 The Centre of the Circle

When I began my journey,
the road was quite narrow
and fear lurked on either side.
I shrank from people who walked paths
so distant they seemed opposite to mine,
and I even called them enemy.
But Love called me on
and the beautiful road grew wider.
Fear was still there but I could see
over its fences, and people on other paths
seemed nearer so that I could call to them
and wish them well as they travelled.
Still, Love called my heart,
and the beautiful road grew so wide
that the boundaries of fear disappeared.
I saw other paths so close to mine
that I wondered how I ever
could have viewed them as alien.
Come, said Love, dragging at my heart,
and now the paths had no separation
and no horizons, only a brightness
that transcended all ways and words.
We did not need to name it,
for in its light, we were all one.

55 The Variety of Being

Oh Holy One, we stand with awe
before the diversity of your creation.
Wherever we look, You are proclaimed, unique
in a million disguises of form and colour,
cloud and water, feather and scale, leaf and stone,
the rough, the smooth, the infinitely big and small,
so much that our eyes are overwhelmed by wonder
and we can take in only one thing at a time.
With such limited vision it is easy to miss
the Oneness that makes up the millions.
Yet each of us is your parable, Oh Holy One,
 a tiny echo of the truth of the multitude,
for each of us is a universe of diversity,
galaxies of cells, living constellations,
planets populated by microscopic creatures
that come and go in us, and yet remain
an inseparable part of the consciousness
of ourselves as individuals.
Oh Holy One, the parable reminds us
that we are more than your story,
more than the creation of your Word,
for when separation falls away,
as the wave fall back into the ocean,
there is only the Oneness of You.

56 The Mystery of Paradox

The instinct for survival is loud in us.
It cries, protect yourself! Don't take risks.
Look after number one before others.
But in the heart, comes a murmur,
put others first and you will escape
from the small prison of self.
Grab what you can! Our instinct shouts.
Surround yourself with security
and fiercely guard your possessions.
Get rid of all this stuff, the heart whispers.
Your house has become so cluttered
that the light no longer comes in.
Fight! Screams the instinct for survival.
Get them before they get you.
Show them that no one puts you down.
Go to them in love, says the heart.
Anger creates anger. War creates war.
Only love bears the fruit of love.
The primal instinct is loud in us
but the voice of the heart is stronger.
Who are you? We ask in prayer.
You have always known me,
says the voice of the heart.
I am the way, the truth
and the greater life.
I am the Christ.

57 Evening Prayer

I give thanks for this day
which covers me like a patchwork quilt,
a day made up of many small pieces,
some colourful and full of celebration,
some patches plain or subdued
and others a bit frayed around the edges,
all of it blessed by the God of Abundance.
Piece by piece, I offer my gratitude,
for the times I noticed the beauty around me,
for smiles given and smiles received,
for the goodness of sun and rain,
the freshness of bread and water,
and the great comfort of friends
who see not pieces but the whole.
For the mistakes in my day,
the patches that need mending tomorrow,
I give God my fullest thanks, for these
are the learning parts of my life
open to growth through infinite grace.
I hold each error with heartfelt gratitude,
and seek ways to make repairs.
It is such a comfort to know
that I am still growing.

Glossary

8.   Haere mai
        haere mai   come/welcome
        kia ora   greeting/good health
        whanau   family
        whakapapa   heritage/lineage
        Hehu Karaiti Jesus Christ

28.   The Oneness of Being
        kauri   large cone-bearing tree

37.   Beauty
        paua   NZ abalone shellfish